chinese

chinese

THE AUTHENTIC TASTE OF CHINA IN DELICIOUSLY SIMPLE RECIPES

foreword by
deh-ta hsiung

LORENZ BOOKS

This edition published by Lorenz Books
an imprint of Anness Publishing Limited
Hermes House, 88-89 Blackfriars Road, London SE1 8HA

This edition distributed in Canada by Raincoast Books
8680 Cambie Street, Vancouver, British Columbia V6P 6M9

ISBN 0-7548-0349-X

A CIP catalogue record for this book is available from the British Library

Publisher Joanna Lorenz
Senior Cookery Editor Linda Fraser
Cookery Editor Anne Hildyard
Designer Nigel Partridge
Illustrations Madeleine David
Photographers Karl Adamson, Edward Allwright, Steve Baxter, James Duncan, Michelle Garrett, Amanda Heywood and Michael Michaels
Recipes Alex Barker, Roz Denny, Rati Fernandez, Christine France, Shirley Gill, Deh-Ta Hsiung, Liz Trigg and Steven Wheeler
Food for photography Elizabeth Wolf-Cohen, Carole Handslip, Wendy Lee and Jane Stevenson
Stylists Madelaine Brehaut, Michelle Garrett, Maria Kelly, Blake Minton and Kirsty Rawlings
Cover *Photography* Nicki Dowey, *Food Stylist* Emma Patmore, *Design* Wilson Harvey Marketing and Design

Previously published as part of the *Classic* cookery series

Printed and bound in Singapore

1 3 5 7 9 10 8 6 4 2

For all recipes, quantities are given in both metric and imperial measures, and, where appropriate, measures are also given in standard cups and spoons. Follow one set, but not a mixture, because they are not interchangeable.

Pictures on frontispiece and pages 2, 7, 8 and 9: Zefa Pictures Ltd.

CONTENTS

Foreword

Chinese cooking is the most popular ethnic food, not just in the West, but also in every other part of the world. Chinese food, with its unique flavours and cooking techniques, has an inherent appeal. It is also both economical and healthy: because most ingredients are cut into small pieces before being cooked very quickly, they retain their natural flavours and nutrients.

Despite all the foreign influences and technological advances which have affected nearly all walks of life in China, the indigenous cuisine remains remarkably resistant to drastic change. Although foreign foodstuffs have been introduced into China for many centuries, they have become integral ingredients in many Chinese dishes.

A Chinese cook abroad can always produce a Chinese meal, even when using only local produce, for the essential "Chineseness" of the food depends entirely on *how* it is prepared and cooked, not *what* ingredients are used.

The most distinctive feature in Chinese cooking is the emphasis on the harmonious blending of colour, aroma, flavour and texture, both in a single dish and in all the dishes that make up a meal. Food preparation is another important element: it is essential that ingredients be cut into uniform shapes and sizes, whether these be small thin slices, shreds or cubes. This is done not only for the sake of the appearance of the finished dish, but also because ingredients of a similar size and shape require about the same amount of cooking time.

40 easy-to-follow recipes from many different regions of China have been selected for this book. I have contributed to the collection myself, and would like to commend all the dishes for you to try at home.

Bon appetit! Or, as we say in China, *Ching, Ching!*

DEH-TA HSIUNG

精神
一元
車厘子
RED CHERRIES

Introduction

China is a vast country. Stretching from the sub-arctic north to the tropical south, the different climatic zones and landscapes have given rise to a number of distinct cuisines, some of which are only now becoming known in the West. While we have become familiar with Cantonese cooking, with its sweet and sour treatment of pork and prawns, and its use of fresh vegetables and fruit, our experience of the cuisine of northern Beijing tends to be limited to Peking duck and Crispy Aromatic Duck (see the recipe on page 32). The coastal

provinces around Shanghai are known for fish dishes, and wheat, rice, soya beans and vegetables are also grown here. In the south-west, in Szechuan, hot and spicy dishes characterize the regional style of cooking.

Cooking methods also vary from province to province. Meat is either cooked slowly by braising or steaming or quickly stir-fried, whereas poultry dishes are either crispy (having been deep-fried) or tender and moist, (having been simmered). Whole fish such as garoupa are often steamed with aromatics such as ginger and spring onions, while seafood, such

as prawns and scallops, are stir-fried briefly so that they retain maximum moisture and flavour. Vegetables play a vital role, and the use of fresh produce is very important in Chinese cooking.

Specialist ingredients include glutinous rice and a wide range of noodles, including egg, rice and cellophane noodles. Protein-rich soya beans are used extensively, in pastes, purées, sauces and the increasingly popular tofu. Soy sauce is now available in various strengths, from the delicately flavoured light soy sauce to the more salty dark variety. Dark soy sauce gives a rich colour to a dish; where it is desirable not to mask natural colours, the lighter sauce is used. Yellow bean sauce and black bean sauce

Dried fish of every variety are on sale at this open-air stall in a street in Macau (far left) while persimmons and pomegranates are some of the exotic fruits on offer at a roadside market (left). On the Li river (above), fishermen set off into a lovely sunset.

are also made from soya beans, but are thicker than soy sauce. Black bean sauce is a special favourite and is often cooked with pork, fish or seafood. Preserved black beans are very salty – they are usually mashed into the sauce at the end of cooking. The range of sauces includes hoi-sin, which has a hot, sweet flavour (excellent as a marinade for spare ribs) and oyster sauce. There is also a red bean paste, which is used as a dip or spread on the pancakes served with Peking duck, and chilli paste, which is made from chillies, soya beans, salt, sugar and flour.

Tofu – pressed soya bean curd – is available in various forms, from soft to firm, and can be cubed or sliced. Smoked firm tofu is also on sale. Specialist oils, like the nutty sesame oil and the fiery chilli oil, can also be used to add flavour to a dish, but, as the foreword to this book suggests, harmony is very important in the composition of both single dishes and entire Chinese meals. No sauce should dominate, and colours, flavours, aromas and textures should be in balance.

Chinese food is easy to prepare at home, especially now that the ingredients needed are so readily available. Even the smallest supermarket carries an extensive range, so familiarize yourself with this book, get out your wok and steamer, and you will soon be enjoying the diverse tastes and authentic flavours offered by *Classic Chinese*.

Marbled Quail's Eggs

Hard-boiled quail's eggs reboiled in smoky China tea assume a pretty marbled effect. Dip them into a fragrant spicy salt and hand them round with drinks, or serve them as a starter. Szechuan peppercorns can be bought from oriental food shops.

Ingredients

12 quail's eggs
600ml/1 pint/2½ cups strong lapsang souchong tea
15ml/1 tbsp dark soy sauce
15ml/1 tbsp dry sherry
2 whole star anise
curly endive, ground Szechuan peppercorns and sea salt, to serve

Serves 4–6

1 Place the quail's eggs in a saucepan of cold water and bring to the boil. Time them for 2 minutes from the moment when the water comes to the boil.

2 Transfer the eggs from the pan to a colander and run them under cold water to cool. Tap the shells all over so they are crazed, but do not peel the eggs.

Cook's Tip

Szechuan peppercorns are dried reddish brown berries from a shrub native to Szechuan. They are not so hot as the true peppercorn, but have a numbing effect and a distinctive aroma. They are roasted, ground, and the husks discarded before use.

3 In a large saucepan, bring the tea to the boil, then add the soy sauce, sherry and star anise. Add the eggs and boil again for about 15 minutes, partially covered, so the liquid does not boil dry.

4 Remove the eggs from the pan. When they are cool, peel and arrange on a small platter lined with curly endive.

5 Mix the ground Szechuan peppercorns with an equal quantity of salt and place the mixture in a small dish to serve with the eggs.

GARLIC MUSHROOMS

Tofu is high in protein and very low in fat, so it is a very useful food to keep handy for quick and healthy meals and snacks like this one.

INGREDIENTS

8 large open-cup mushrooms
3 spring onions, sliced lengthways
1 garlic clove, crushed
30ml/2 tbsp oyster sauce
275g/10oz carton marinated tofu, cut into small dice
200g/7oz can sweetcorn, drained
10ml/2 tsp sesame oil
salt and ground black pepper
spring onion strips, to garnish

SERVES 4

COOK'S TIP
If you prefer, omit the oyster sauce and use light soy sauce instead.

1 Preheat the oven to 200°C/400°F/Gas 6. Set aside the mushroom cups and finely chop the stalks. Place the stalks in a bowl, add the spring onions and garlic and pour over the oyster sauce. Stir to mix.

2 Dry the marinated tofu and add it with the sweetcorn to the mushroom mixture, season with salt and pepper, then stir to combine.

3 Place the mushroom cups, open-side up, on a plate or chopping board and divide the stuffing mixture among them.

4 Brush the edges of the mushrooms with the oil. Arrange the mushrooms in a baking dish and bake for 12–15 minutes, until the mushrooms are just tender, then serve garnished with the spring onion strips.

Prawn and Sweetcorn Soup

This is a very quick and easy soup, made in minutes. If you are using frozen prawns, defrost them first before adding them to the soup.

Ingredients

2.5ml/½ tsp sesame or sunflower oil
2 spring onions, thinly sliced
1 garlic clove, crushed
600ml/1 pint/2½ cups chicken stock
425g/15oz can creamed sweetcorn
225g/8oz/1¼ cups cooked, peeled prawns
5ml/1 tsp green chilli paste or chilli sauce (optional)
salt and ground black pepper
fresh coriander leaves, to garnish

Serves 4

1 Heat the oil in a large heavy-based saucepan and sauté the spring onions and garlic over a medium heat for 1 minute, until softened, but not browned.

2 Stir in the chicken stock, creamed sweetcorn, prawns and chilli paste or sauce, if using.

3 Bring the soup to the boil, stirring occasionally. Season to taste, then ladle the soup into warmed individual bowls. Serve at once, sprinkled with fresh coriander leaves to garnish.

Cook's Tip

If creamed sweetcorn is not available, use ordinary canned sweetcorn instead. Purée it in a blender or food processor for a few seconds, until it is creamy but still has some texture left and use as instructed in the recipe.

Mini Spring Rolls

Eat these light crispy parcels with your fingers. If you like slightly spicier food, sprinkle them with a little cayenne pepper before serving.

INGREDIENTS

1 green chilli
75g/3oz cooked chicken breast
120ml/4fl oz/½ cup vegetable oil
1 small onion, finely chopped
1 clove garlic, crushed
1 small carrot, cut into fine matchsticks
1 spring onion, finely sliced
1 small red pepper, seeded and cut into fine matchsticks
25g/1oz beansprouts
5ml/1tsp sesame oil
4 large sheets filo pastry
1 egg white, lightly beaten
fresh chives, to garnish (optional)
light soy sauce, to serve

MAKES 20

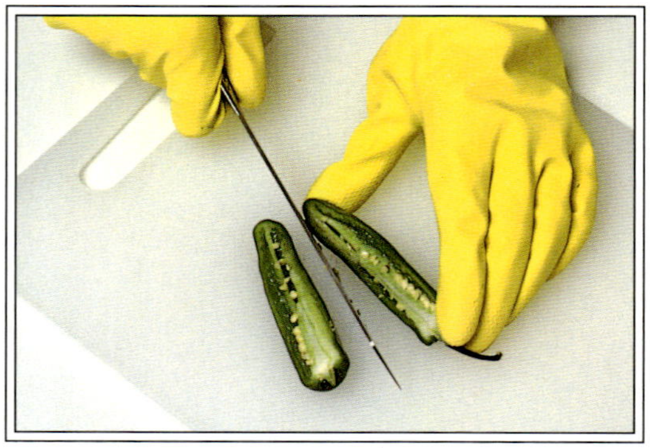

1 Carefully remove the seeds from the chilli and chop finely, wearing rubber gloves to protect your hands, if necessary, as chillies can burn your skin. Avoid all contact with your eyes.

2 Using a sharp knife, slice the chicken breast into thin strips. Heat a wok, then add 30ml/2 tbsp of the vegetable oil. When it is hot, add the onion, garlic and chilli and stir-fry for 1 minute. Add the chicken strips to the wok and fry over a high heat, stirring constantly until they are browned all over.

3 Add the carrot, spring onion and red pepper to the wok and stir-fry for about 2 minutes. Add the beansprouts, stir in the sesame oil, then remove the wok from the heat and leave the mixture to cool.

4 Cut each sheet of filo pastry into five short strips. Place a small amount of the filling at one end of each strip, leaving a small border at the edges, then fold in the long sides and roll up the pastry.

5 Seal and glaze the parcels with the egg white, then chill them, uncovered, for 15 minutes before frying.

6 Wipe out the wok with kitchen paper, reheat it, and add the remaining vegetable oil. When the oil is hot, add the rolls in batches and stir-fry until they are crisp and golden brown. Drain them on kitchen paper. Garnish with chives and serve with light soy sauce for dipping.

STIR-FRIED SEAFOOD

A colourful and delicious dish from South-East China, combining prawns, squid, and scallops. The squid may be replaced by another fish, or omitted altogether.

INGREDIENTS

115g/4oz squid, cleaned
4–6 fresh scallops
115g/4oz uncooked prawns
½ egg white
15ml/1 tbsp cornflour, mixed with a little water
2–3 celery sticks
1 small red pepper, cored and seeded
2 small carrots
300ml/½ pint/1¼ cups oil
2.5ml/½ tsp finely chopped fresh root ginger
1 spring onion, cut into short sections
5ml/1 tsp salt
2.5ml/½ tsp light brown sugar
15ml/1 tbsp Chinese rice wine or dry sherry
15ml/1 tbsp light soy sauce
5ml/1 tsp hot bean sauce
30ml/2 tbsp chicken stock
few drops of sesame oil, to serve

SERVES 4

1 Open up the squid and, using a sharp knife, score the inside in a criss-cross pattern. Cut the squid into 1cm/½in pieces. Soak the squid in a bowl of boiling water until all the pieces curl up; rinse in cold water and drain.

2 Cut each scallop into 3–4 slices. Peel the prawns and cut each one in half lengthways. In a bowl, mix the scallops and prawns with the egg white and cornflour paste until well blended.

3 Cut the celery, red pepper and carrots into 1–2.5cm/½–1in slices.

4 Heat a wok, then add the oil. When it is medium-hot, add the seafood and stir-fry for about 30–40 seconds. Remove with a large slotted spoon and drain.

5 Pour off the excess oil, leaving about 30ml/2 tbsp in the wok, and add the vegetables with the ginger and spring onion. Stir-fry for about 1 minute.

6 Return the seafood to the wok, stir for another 30–40 seconds, then stir in the salt, sugar, wine or sherry, soy sauce and hot bean sauce. Add the stock and stir for about 1 minute. Serve sprinkled with sesame oil.

Red and White Prawns

The Chinese name for this dish is Yuan Yang Prawns. Pairs of mandarin ducks are also known as *Yuan Yang,* or love birds, because they are always seen together. They symbolize affection and happiness.

Ingredients

450g/1lb uncooked prawns
pinch of salt
½ egg white
15ml/1 tbsp cornflour, mixed with a little water
175g/6oz mange-touts
600ml/1 pint/2½ cups vegetable oil
2.5ml/½ tsp salt
5ml/1 tsp light brown sugar
15ml/1 tbsp finely chopped spring onions
5ml/1 tsp finely chopped fresh root ginger
15ml/1 tbsp light soy sauce
15ml/1 tbsp Chinese rice wine or dry sherry
5ml/1 tsp hot bean sauce
15ml/1 tbsp tomato purée

Serves 4–6

1 Peel and de-vein the prawns, and mix with the salt, egg white and cornflour paste. Top and tail the mange-touts.

2 Heat a wok, then add 30–45ml/ 2–3 tbsp of the oil. When it is hot, add the mange-touts and stir-fry for about 1 minute, then add the salt and sugar and continue stirring for 1 further minute. Remove the mange-touts with a slotted spoon and place in the centre of a warmed serving platter.

3 Heat the remaining oil, partially cook the prawns for 1 minute, remove, and drain on kitchen paper.

4 Pour off the excess oil, leaving about 15ml/1 tbsp in the wok, and add the spring onions, ginger and prawns. Stir-fry for 1 minute, then add the soy sauce and wine or sherry. Blend well and place half of the prawns at one end of the platter.

5 Add the hot bean sauce and tomato purée to the remaining prawns. Blend well and place the "red" prawns at the other end of the platter. Serve at once.

STEAMED FISH WITH GINGER

Any firm-fleshed fish with a delicate taste, such as salmon or turbot, can be cooked by this method. The sweet taste of ginger combined with spring onions makes this dish a firm favourite on mainland China.

INGREDIENTS

1 sea bass, trout or striped mullet, weighing about 675g/1½lb, cleaned
2.5ml/½ tsp salt
15ml/1 tbsp sesame oil
2–3 spring onions, cut in half lengthways
30ml/2 tbsp light soy sauce
30ml/2 tbsp Chinese rice wine or dry sherry
15ml/1 tbsp finely grated fresh root ginger
30ml/2 tbsp vegetable oil
finely shredded spring onions, to garnish

SERVES 4–6

1 Using a sharp knife, score both sides of the fish as far down as the bone, making several diagonal cuts about 2.5cm/1in apart. Rub the fish all over, inside and out, with salt and sesame oil.

2 Scatter the spring onions evenly over a heatproof platter and place the fish on top. Blend the soy sauce and wine or sherry with the ginger and pour over the fish.

3 Place the platter in a steamer over boiling water (or inside a wok on a rack), and steam vigorously, covered, for about 12–15 minutes until the fish is cooked *(left)*.

4 Heat the oil in a small saucepan; remove the platter from the steamer, place the shredded spring onions on top of the fish, then pour the hot oil along the whole length of the fish. Serve immediately.

PRAWN FU-YUNG

This is a very colourful dish that is simple to make. Most of the preparation can be done well in advance. It comes from the south of China.

INGREDIENTS

3 eggs, beaten, reserving 5ml/1 tsp of egg white
5ml/1 tsp salt
15ml/1 tbsp finely chopped spring onions
45–60ml/3–4 tbsp vegetable oil
225g/8oz uncooked prawns, peeled
10ml/2 tsp cornflour, mixed with a little water
175g/6oz peas
15ml/1 tbsp Chinese rice wine or dry sherry

SERVES 4

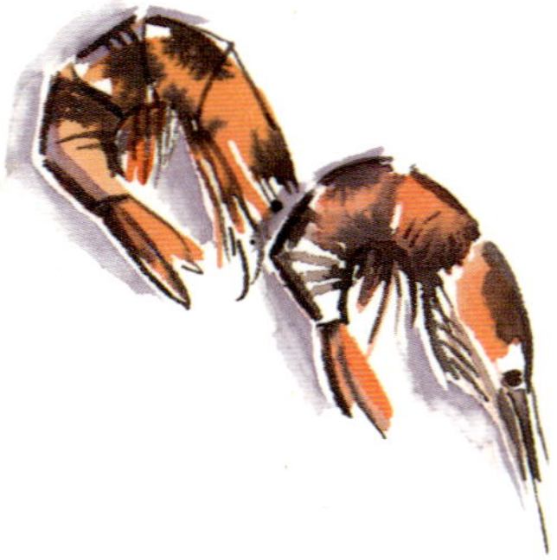

1 Beat the eggs with a pinch of the salt, and a little of the spring onion. In a wok, scramble the eggs in a little oil over a moderate heat. Remove and reserve.

2 Mix the prawns with a little of the salt, the egg white, and cornflour paste. Heat the oil in a wok. When it is hot, add the peas and stir-fry for 30 seconds. Add the prawns.

3 Add the spring onions, and stir-fry for 1 further minute, then stir the mixture into the scrambled egg with the last of the salt and the wine or sherry. Blend well and serve immediately.

FIVE-SPICE FISH

Chinese mixtures of spicy, sweet and sour flavours are particularly successful with fish, and dinner is ready in minutes.

INGREDIENTS

4 white fish fillets, such as cod, haddock or flounder, about 175g/6oz each
5ml/1 tsp five-spice powder
20ml/4 tsp cornflour
15ml/1 tbsp sesame or sunflower oil
3 spring onions, finely sliced
5ml/1 tsp finely chopped fresh root ginger
150g/5oz button mushrooms, sliced
115g/4oz baby sweetcorn, sliced
30ml/2 tbsp soy sauce
45ml/3 tbsp dry sherry or apple juice
5ml/1 tsp sugar
salt and ground black pepper
stir-fried vegetables, to serve

SERVES 4

1 Toss the fish fillets in the five-spice powder and cornflour to coat.

2 Heat the oil in a wok or frying pan and stir-fry the spring onions, ginger, mushrooms and sweetcorn for about 1 minute. Add the fish fillets and cook for 2–3 minutes, turning once.

3 In a small bowl, mix together the soy sauce, sherry or juice and sugar, then pour over the fish. Simmer for 2 minutes, season, then serve immediately with stir-fried vegetables.

BRAISED FISH WITH MUSHROOMS

This is a version of the French *filets de sole bonne femme* (sole with mushrooms and wine sauce), with oriental flavours.

INGREDIENTS

450g/1lb fillets of lemon sole or plaice
½ egg white
30ml/2 tbsp cornflour, mixed with a little water
600ml/1 pint/2½ cups vegetable oil
15ml/1 tbsp finely chopped spring onions
2.5ml/½ tsp finely chopped fresh root ginger
115g/4oz white mushrooms, thinly sliced
5ml/1 tsp light brown sugar
15ml/1 tbsp light soy sauce
30ml/2 tbsp Chinese rice wine or dry sherry
15ml/1 tbsp brandy
120ml/4fl oz/½ cup chicken stock
salt
few drops of sesame oil, to serve

SERVES 4

1 Trim off the soft bones along the edge of the fish, but leave the skin on. Cut each fillet into bite-size pieces. Put a little salt, the egg white and about half of the cornflour paste into a small bowl and mix together. Coat the fish pieces in the mixture.

2 Heat the oil in a wok until medium-hot, add the fish pieces one at a time and stir gently so they do not stick. Remove after about 1 minute and drain. Pour off all but 30ml/2 tbsp of oil. Stir-fry the spring onions, ginger and mushrooms for 1 minute.

3 Add the sugar, light soy sauce, rice wine or sherry, the brandy and stock and bring to the boil. Add the fish pieces and braise for 1 minute. Thicken with the remaining cornflour paste and sprinkle with sesame oil. Serve immediately.

Stir-Fried Beef with Orange and Ginger

Stir-frying uses the minimum of fat and it's also one of the quickest ways to cook, but you do need to choose very tender meat.

Ingredients

450g/1lb lean beef rump, fillet or sirloin cut into thin strips
finely grated rind and juice of 1 orange
15ml/1 tbsp light soy sauce
5ml/1 tsp cornflour
2.5cm/1in piece fresh root ginger, finely chopped
10ml/2 tsp sesame oil
1 large carrot, cut into thin strips
2 spring onions, thinly sliced
rice noodles or boiled rice, to serve

Serves 4

1 Place the beef strips in a bowl and sprinkle over the orange rind and juice. Cover and leave to marinate for at least 30 minutes, stirring from time to time.

2 Drain the marinade from the meat and reserve the marinade. Mix the meat with the soy sauce, cornflour and ginger.

Cook's Tip

To extract the maximum amount of juice from an orange, warm it for a short while in the oven, then roll it backwards and forwards with your hand before squeezing.

3 Heat the sesame oil in a wok or large frying pan. When it is hot, add the beef strips and stir-fry for 1 minute until they are lightly coloured. Add the carrot strips and stir-fry for a further 2–3 minutes.

4 Stir in the sliced spring onions and the reserved marinade, then cook over a medium heat, stirring constantly, until the sauce is boiling, thickened and glossy. Serve the stir-fried beef immediately, accompanied by a serving of rice noodles, or just plain boiled rice.

SWEET AND SOUR LAMB

This recipe from the Imperial kitchens of the Manchu Dynasty is perhaps a forerunner of today's favourite sweet and sour pork.

INGREDIENTS

350–400g/12–14oz boneless leg of lamb
15ml/1 tbsp yellow bean sauce
vegetable oil, for deep-frying
2.5ml/½ tsp finely chopped fresh root ginger
½ cucumber, thinly sliced
15ml/1 tbsp light soy sauce
15ml/1 tbsp Chinese rice wine or dry sherry
30ml/2 tbsp rice vinegar
30ml/2 tbsp light brown sugar
45–60ml/3–4 tbsp chicken stock or water
15ml/1 tbsp cornflour, mixed with a little water
2.5ml/½ tsp sesame oil

SERVES 4

1 Cut the lamb into thin 2.5cm/1in slices. Place the lamb in a bowl, and mix with the yellow bean sauce. Leave to marinate for 35–40 minutes, stirring from time to time.

2 Heat the oil in a wok, and deep-fry the lamb for about 30–40 seconds or until the colour changes. Remove with a slotted spoon and drain well *(left)*.

3 Pour off the excess oil, leaving about 7.5ml/½ tbsp. Add the ginger, cucumber, soy sauce, wine or sherry, vinegar, sugar, stock, cornflour paste and sesame oil and stir until smooth. Add the lamb, blend well, and serve immediately.

GINGER PORK WITH BLACK BEAN SAUCE

The combination of the sweetness of peppers and the saltiness of preserved black beans gives this dish a wonderful, distinctive flavour.

INGREDIENTS

350g/12oz pork fillet
1 garlic clove, crushed
15ml/1 tbsp grated fresh root ginger
90ml/6 tbsp chicken stock
30ml/2 tbsp dry sherry
15ml/1 tbsp light soy sauce
5ml/1 tsp sugar
10ml/2 tsp cornflour
45ml/3 tbsp groundnut oil
2 yellow peppers, seeded and cut into strips
2 red peppers, seeded and cut into strips
1 bunch spring onions, sliced diagonally
45ml/3 tbsp preserved black beans, coarsely chopped
fresh coriander, to garnish (optional)

SERVES 4

1 Cut the pork into thin slices across the grain of the meat. Put the slices into a bowl and mix them with the garlic and ginger. Leave to marinate at room temperature for 15 minutes.

2 Blend together the stock, sherry, soy sauce, sugar and cornflour in a small bowl, then set the sauce mixture aside.

3 Heat the oil in a wok or large frying pan, add the marinated pork and stir-fry for 2–3 minutes. Add the peppers and spring onions and stir-fry for a further 2 minutes *(left)*. Add the beans and sauce mixture and cook, stirring, until thick. Serve hot, garnished with fresh coriander, if using.

MU SHU PORK WITH EGGS AND MUSHROOMS

In Chinese *Mu Shu* is the name for a bright yellow flower. Traditionally, this dish is served as a filling wrapped in thin pancakes, but it can also be served on its own with plain rice.

INGREDIENTS

15g/½oz dried wood-ear mushrooms
175–225g/6–8oz pork tenderloin
225g/8oz Chinese cabbage
115g/4oz canned bamboo shoots, drained
2 spring onions
3 eggs
5ml/1 tsp salt
60ml/4 tbsp vegetable oil
15ml/1 tbsp light soy sauce
15ml/1 tbsp Chinese rice wine or dry sherry
few drops of sesame oil, to serve

SERVES 4

1 Soak the mushrooms in a bowl of cold water for 25–30 minutes, then rinse thoroughly and discard any hard stalks. Drain the mushrooms, then thinly slice. Cut the pork into matchstick pieces. Thinly shred the Chinese cabbage, bamboo shoots and spring onions.

2 Break the eggs into a bowl, add a pinch of salt, and beat. Heat a little oil in a wok, add the eggs and stir and turn gently until lightly scrambled but not at all dry. Remove, set aside and keep warm.

3 Heat the remaining oil in the wok, add the pork and stir-fry for about 1 minute, or until the colour changes. Add the mushrooms, Chinese cabbage, bamboo shoots and spring onions and stir-fry for 1 further minute, then add the remaining salt, the soy sauce, and wine or sherry.

4 Stir-fry the vegetables for 1 further minute before returning the scrambled eggs to the wok. Break up the eggs and blend in well. Sprinkle with sesame oil and serve immediately.

Crispy Aromatic Duck

Because this dish is often served with pancakes, spring onions, cucumber and duck sauce or plum sauce, many people mistakenly think it is Peking duck. This recipe, however, uses quite a different cooking method. The result is just as crispy but the delightful aroma makes this dish particularly distinctive. Thin pancakes are widely available from Chinese supermarkets and delicatessens.

INGREDIENTS

1 oven-ready duckling, weighing about 1.75–2.25kg/4½–5lb
10ml/2 tsp salt
5–6 whole star anise
15ml/1 tbsp Szechuan peppercorns
5ml/1 tsp cloves
2–3 cinnamon sticks
3–4 spring onions
3–4 slices fresh root ginger, unpeeled
75–90ml/5–6 tbsp Chinese rice wine or dry sherry
vegetable oil, for deep-frying
lettuce leaves, to garnish
12–16 thin pancakes, plum sauce, ½ bunch shredded spring onions, ½ cucumber cut into matchstick strips, to serve

SERVES 6–8

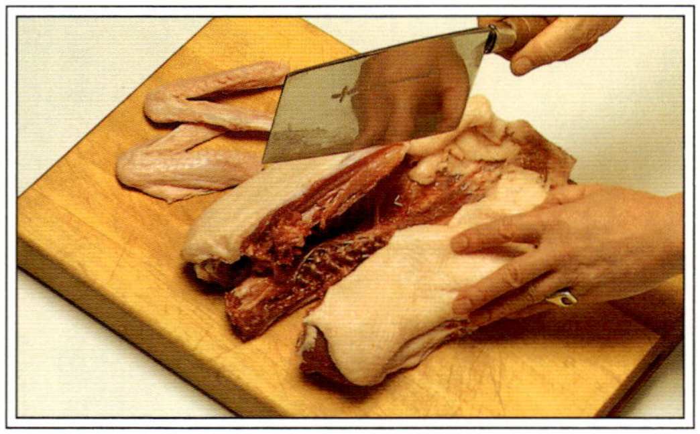

1 Remove the wings from the duck. Split the body in half down the backbone. Rub salt all over the two duck halves, taking care to rub it well in. Place the duck in a dish with the spices, the spring onions, root ginger and rice wine or sherry. Leave the duck to marinate for at least 4–6 hours, turning occasionally.

2 Steam the duck vigorously with the marinade for 3–4 hours (longer if possible), then remove from the cooking liquid and leave to cool, covered, for at least 5–6 hours. The duck must be completely cold and dry or the skin will not be crispy.

3 Heat the oil in a wok until smoking, place the duck pieces in the oil, skin-side down, and deep-fry for 5–6 minutes or until crisp and brown, turning just once at the very last moment.

4 Remove the duck from the wok with a slotted spoon and drain on kitchen paper. Arrange the lettuce leaves on a large platter. To serve, place the duck on the lettuce and remove from the bone at the table or before serving. Each guest places a few pieces of meat on a pancake, adds some sauce, spring onion and cucumber, then rolls up the pancake.

"Kung Po" Chicken – Szechuan Style

Kung Po was the name of a court official in Szechuan; his cook created this dish. Omit some or all of the chillies for a less spicy dish.

Ingredients

350g/12oz chicken thighs, skinned and boned
1.5ml/¼ tsp salt
½ egg white, lightly beaten
10ml/2 tsp cornflour, mixed with water
1 green pepper, cored and seeded
60ml/4 tbsp vegetable oil
3–4 whole dried red chillies, soaked in water for 10 minutes
1 spring onion, cut into short sections
few small pieces of fresh root ginger, peeled
15ml/1 tbsp sweet bean paste or hoi-sin sauce
5ml/1 tsp hot bean paste
15ml/1 tbsp Chinese rice wine or dry sherry
115g/4oz/1 cup roasted cashew nuts and a few drops of sesame oil, to serve

Serves 4

1 Cut the chicken into 1cm/½in cubes. In a bowl, mix the chicken with the salt, egg white and cornflour paste. Cut the green pepper into squares about the same size as the chicken cubes.

2 Heat a wok, then add the oil. When it is hot, add the chicken cubes and stir-fry for about 1 minute, or until the colour changes. Remove the chicken from the wok with a slotted spoon and keep warm.

3 Add the green pepper, soaked red chillies, spring onion and ginger and stir-fry for about 1 minute.

4 Add the chicken to the wok with the sweet bean paste or hoi-sin sauce, hot bean paste and wine or sherry. Blend thoroughly and cook for 1 further minute. Finally stir in the cashew nuts and sesame oil. Transfer to a warmed serving platter and serve immediately.

Chicken and Vegetable Stir-fry

Make this quick supper dish a little hotter and spicier by adding either more fresh root ginger or more oyster sauce, if you wish.

Ingredients

rind of ½ lemon
1cm/½in piece of fresh root ginger
1 large garlic clove
30ml/2 tbsp sunflower oil
275g/10oz lean chicken, thinly sliced
½ red pepper, seeded and sliced
½ green pepper, seeded and sliced
4 spring onions, chopped
2 carrots, cut into matchsticks
115g/4oz fine French beans
30ml/2 tbsp oyster sauce
pinch of sugar
25g/1oz/¼ cup salted peanuts, lightly crushed
salt and ground black pepper
fresh coriander leaves, to garnish
rice, to serve

Serves 4

1 Thinly slice the lemon rind. Peel and chop the ginger and garlic. Heat the oil in a frying pan or wok over a high heat. Add the lemon rind, ginger and garlic, and stir-fry for 30 seconds until brown.

2 Add the chicken and stir-fry for about 2 minutes. Add the vegetables *(left)* and stir-fry for 4–5 minutes, until the chicken is cooked and the vegetables are tender.

3 Finally stir in the oyster sauce, sugar, peanuts and seasoning to taste and stir-fry for another minute to mix and blend well. Serve at once, sprinkled with the coriander leaves and accompanied with rice.

CHICKEN WITH CHINESE VEGETABLES

The chicken in this recipe can be replaced by almost any other meat, such as pork, beef or liver – or you can even use prawns, if you prefer.

INGREDIENTS

225–275g/8–10oz chicken, boned and skinned
5ml/1 tsp salt
½ egg white, lightly beaten
10ml/2 tsp cornflour, mixed with a little water
60ml/4 tbsp vegetable oil
6–8 small dried shiitake mushrooms, soaked
115g/4oz sliced bamboo shoots, drained
115g/4oz mange-touts, trimmed
1 spring onion, cut into short sections
a few small pieces fresh root ginger, peeled
5ml/1 tsp light brown sugar
15ml/1 tbsp light soy sauce
15ml/1 tbsp Chinese rice wine or dry sherry
few drops of sesame oil, to serve

SERVES 4

1 Cut the chicken into thin 2.5cm/1in slices. In a bowl, mix a pinch of the salt with the egg white and cornflour paste.

2 Heat a wok, then add the oil. When it is hot, add the chicken slices and stir-fry over a medium heat for about 30 seconds, then, using a slotted spoon, transfer to a plate and keep warm.

3 Add the mushrooms, bamboo shoots, mange-touts, spring onion and ginger and stir-fry over a high heat for about 1 minute. Add the salt, sugar, and chicken. Blend together, then add the soy sauce and wine or sherry. Stir a few more times, then sprinkle with the sesame oil and serve.

STIR-FRIED TURKEY WITH MANGE-TOUTS

The crunchiness of the mange-touts, water chestnuts, spring onions and cashew nuts gives this turkey dish an interesting texture.

INGREDIENTS

30ml/2 tbsp sesame oil
90ml/6 tbsp lemon juice
1 garlic clove, crushed
1cm/½in piece fresh root ginger, peeled and grated
5ml/1 tsp clear honey
450ml/1lb turkey fillets, cut into strips
115g/4oz mange-touts, trimmed
30ml/2 tbsp groundnut oil
50g/2oz/½ cup cashew nuts
6 spring onions, cut into strips
225g/8oz can water chestnuts, drained and thinly sliced
salt
saffron rice, to serve

SERVES 4

1 Mix together the sesame oil, lemon juice, garlic, ginger and honey in a shallow non-metallic dish. Add the turkey and mix well. Cover and leave to marinate for 3–4 hours stirring occasionally.

2 Blanch the mange-touts in boiling salted water for 1 minute. Drain and refresh under cold running water.

3 Drain the marinade from the turkey strips and reserve the marinade. Heat the groundnut oil in a wok or large frying pan, add the cashew nuts and stir-fry for about 1–2 minutes until golden brown. Using a slotted spoon, remove the cashew nuts from the wok and set them aside.

4 Add the turkey strips to the wok and stir-fry for 3–4 minutes, until they are golden brown on all sides. Add the spring onions, mange-touts and water chestnuts and pour in the reserved marinade. Cook for a few minutes, until the turkey is tender and the sauce is bubbling and hot.

5 Return the nuts to the wok and stir in. Transfer to a warmed serving platter and serve immediately, with saffron rice.

Soy-Braised Chicken

This dish can be served hot or cold. Soy sauce is a vital ingredient in Chinese cooking. Light soy sauce is thinner and saltier than dark.

Ingredients

1 whole chicken, weighing about 1.5kg/3–3½lb
15ml/1 tbsp ground Szechuan peppercorns
30ml/2 tbsp finely chopped fresh root ginger
45ml/3 tbsp light soy sauce
30ml/2 tbsp dark soy sauce
45ml/3 tbsp Chinese rice wine or sherry
15ml/1 tbsp light brown sugar
vegetable oil, for deep-frying
600ml/1 pint/2½ cups chicken stock or water
10ml/2 tsp salt
25g/1oz/2 tbsp sugar
lettuce leaves, to garnish

Serves 6–8

1 Rub the chicken, both inside and out, with the Szechuan pepper and ginger. Marinate the bird with the soy sauces, wine or sherry and sugar for 3 hours, turning the bird several times.

2 Heat a wok, then add the oil. When it is hot, add the chicken, reserving the marinade, and deep-fry for 5–6 minutes, or until brown all over.

3 Remove and drain. Pour off the excess oil, add the marinade with the stock or water, salt and the sugar and bring to the boil. Return the chicken to the wok and braise in the sauce, covered, for 35–40 minutes, turning once or twice.

4 Remove the chicken and let it cool a little before chopping it into about 30 bite-size pieces. Arrange the chicken pieces on a bed of lettuce leaves, then pour some of the sauce over and serve at once. Use the remaining sauce another time.

POK CHOI AND MUSHROOM STIR-FRY

Try to buy all the mushrooms, if you can, as the variety of flavours gives great subtlety to the finished dish; the oyster and shiitake mushrooms have particularly distinctive flavours.

INGREDIENTS

4 dried black Chinese mushrooms
450g/1lb pok choi
50g/2oz oyster mushrooms
50g/2oz shiitake mushrooms
15ml/1 tbsp vegetable oil
1 garlic clove, crushed
30ml/2 tbsp oyster sauce

SERVES 4

COOK'S TIP

Pok or pak choi is a type of cabbage with long thin stems and dark green leaves. Bok choi can be used instead. The leaves are crisper but the flavour is very similar.

1 Put the dried black Chinese mushrooms into a small bowl and pour over 150ml/¼ pint/⅔ cup boiling water. Leave for about 15 minutes to let them soften.

2 Meanwhile, tear the pok choi into bite-size pieces with your fingers. Using a sharp knife, halve any large oyster or shiitake mushrooms, using a sharp knife.

3 Strain the Chinese mushrooms. Heat the wok, then add the oil. When hot, stir-fry the garlic until softened but not coloured.

4 Add the pok choi and stir-fry for about 1 minute. Mix in all the mushrooms and stir-fry for 1 minute. Finally, add the oyster sauce, toss well and serve immediately.

VARIATION

Braise the mushrooms in a well-flavoured sauce. Omit the pok choi. Heat 15ml/1 tbsp oil in a wok, add a selection of mushrooms and stir-fry for 1 minute, then add 30ml/2 tbsp each of dark soy sauce, Chinese rice wine or dry sherry and sugar, 5ml/1 tsp sesame oil and 300ml/½ pint/1¼ cups chicken or vegetable stock. Reduce the heat and braise, stirring for 5–7 minutes until the liquid has almost evaporated.

Stir-Fried Mixed Vegetables

When selecting different items for a dish, never mix ingredients indiscriminately. In their cooking, as in all things, the Chinese aim to achieve a harmonious balance of colour and texture.

Ingredients

225g/8oz Chinese cabbage
115g/4oz baby sweetcorn
115g/4oz broccoli
1 large or 2 small carrots
60ml/4 tbsp vegetable oil
5ml/1 tsp salt
5ml/1 tsp light brown sugar
chicken stock or water, if necessary
15ml/1 tbsp light soy sauce
few drops of sesame oil (optional)

Serves 4

1 Cut the Chinese cabbage into thick slices. Cut the sweetcorn lengthways, if wished. Separate the broccoli into florets and slice the carrots diagonally.

2 Heat the oil in a wok, add the Chinese cabbage, sweetcorn, broccoli and carrots and stir-fry for about 2 minutes.

3 Add the salt and sugar, and a little stock or water, if necessary, so the vegetables do not dry out, and continue stirring for another minute (*left*). Add the soy sauce and sesame oil, if using. Blend well into the vegetable mixture and serve immediately.

Crispy Seaweed

In northern China they use a special kind of seaweed for this dish, but spring greens, shredded very finely, make a very good alternative. Serve either as a starter or as a side-dish.

INGREDIENTS

225g/8oz spring greens
groundnut or corn oil, for deep-frying
1.5ml/¼ tsp salt
10ml/2 tsp soft light brown sugar
30–45ml/2–3 tbsp flaked toasted almonds, to garnish

SERVES 4

1 Cut out and discard any tough stalks from the spring greens. Place about six leaves on top of each other and roll up tightly. Using a sharp knife, slice across into very thin shreds. Lay on a tray and leave to dry for about 2 hours.

2 Heat about 5–7.5cm/2–3in of oil in a heavy saucepan or wok to 190°C/375°F. Carefully place a handful of the leaves in the oil – it will bubble and spit for about the first 10 seconds and then die down. Deep-fry the leaves for about 45 seconds, or until they are a slightly darker green – do not let the leaves burn.

3 Remove the leaves with a slotted spoon, drain on kitchen paper and transfer to a serving dish. Keep warm in the oven while frying the remainder.

4 When you have deep-fried all the shredded leaves, sprinkle them with the salt and sugar and toss lightly so that they are all thoroughly coated. Garnish with the toasted almonds and serve immediately.

COOK'S TIP

Make sure that your pan is deep enough to allow the oil to bubble up during cooking. The pan should be less than half full.

TOFU AND CRUNCHY VEGETABLES

Tofu, also known as soya bean curd or just bean curd, is best if it is marinated lightly before cooking to add extra flavour. Using smoked tofu makes this dish even tastier.

INGREDIENTS

2 × 225g/8oz cartons smoked tofu, cubed
45ml/3 tbsp soy sauce
30ml/2 tbsp dry sherry or vermouth
15ml/1 tbsp sesame oil
45ml/3 tbsp groundnut or sunflower oil
2 leeks, thinly sliced
2 carrots, cut into sticks
1 large courgette, thinly sliced
115g/4oz baby sweetcorn, halved
115g/4oz button or shiitake mushrooms, sliced
15ml/1 tbsp sesame seeds
egg noodles, to serve

SERVES 4

COOK'S TIP

The secret of successful stir-frying is to have all your ingredients ready prepared before you heat the oil in the wok. Arrange vegetables on separate dishes and measure out sauces, oils and spices.

1 Place the tofu cubes in a large bowl and add the soy sauce, sherry or vermouth and the sesame oil. Stir to mix thoroughly, then cover and leave to marinate in a cool place for at least 30 minutes. Lift the tofu cubes out of the marinade with a slotted spoon, reserving the marinade.

2 Heat the groundnut or sunflower oil in a wok or large frying pan, add the tofu cubes and stir-fry until browned all over. Remove with a slotted spoon and set aside.

3 Stir-fry the leeks, carrots, courgette and baby sweetcorn, stirring and tossing for about 2 minutes. Add the mushrooms and stir-fry for 1 further minute.

4 Return the tofu cubes to the wok and pour in the reserved marinade. Heat until bubbling, then scatter over the sesame seeds. Serve immediately, straight from the wok, with hot noodles tossed in a little sesame oil if liked.

Braised Vegetables

The original recipe calls for no fewer than 18 different ingredients to represent the 18 Buddhas. Later, this was reduced to eight, but nowadays anything between four and six items is regarded as more than sufficient.

Ingredients

10g/¼oz dried wood-ear mushrooms
75g/3oz straw mushrooms, drained
75g/3oz sliced bamboo shoots, drained
50g/2oz mange-touts
225g/8oz tofu
175g/6oz Chinese cabbage
45–60ml/3–4 tbsp vegetable oil
5ml/1 tsp salt
2.5ml/½ tsp light brown sugar
15ml/1 tbsp light soy sauce
few drops of sesame oil (optional)

Serves 4

1 Soak the wood-ear mushrooms in cold water for 20–25 minutes, then rinse and discard the hard stalks, if any. Cut the straw mushrooms in half lengthways; if large cut in pieces, if small keep them whole. Rinse and drain the bamboo shoot slices. Top and tail the mange-touts. Cut the tofu into about 12 small pieces. Cut the cabbage into pieces about the same size as the mange-touts.

2 Harden the tofu pieces by placing them in a saucepan of boiling water for about 2 minutes. Remove and drain.

3 Heat the oil in a wok or frying pan. When it is hot, add the tofu pieces and lightly brown on all sides. Remove with a slotted spoon and keep warm.

4 Add the wood-ear and straw mushrooms, bamboo shoots, mange-touts and Chinese cabbage to the wok or frying pan and stir-fry for about 1½ minutes, then add the tofu pieces, salt, sugar and soy sauce. Continue stirring for 1 further minute, then cover and braise for 2–3 minutes. Sprinkle with sesame oil, if using, transfer to a warmed platter and serve.

Cook's Tip

When using dried mushrooms, first rinse them under cold running water to remove any grit, then soak in a bowl with water to cover by 5cm/2in.

STIR-FRIED BRUSSELS SPROUTS

An interesting way to cook Brussels sprouts, this method works equally well with shredded green cabbage. It is a recipe which also goes very well with European meals.

INGREDIENTS

450g/1lb Brussels sprouts, shredded
5ml/1 tsp sesame or sunflower oil
2 spring onions, sliced
2.5ml/½ tsp five-spice powder
15ml/1 tbsp light soy sauce
sliced spring onions, to garnish

SERVES 4

1 Trim the Brussels sprouts and remove any loose or yellowing leaves, then shred them finely, either using a large sharp knife or in a food processor.

2 Heat a wok or frying pan and then add the oil. When it is hot, add the Brussels sprouts and spring onions, and stir-fry for about 2 minutes, without letting the vegetables brown.

3 Stir in the five-spice powder and soy sauce (*left*), then cook, stirring, for a further 2–3 minutes, until just tender. Serve at once, garnished with the sliced spring onions.

SEAFOOD CHOW MEIN

Chow mein is a Chinese-American dish in which a combination of seafood, chicken and vegetables are cooked separately and then combined with stir-fried noodles. This basic recipe can be adapted according to taste, using different items for the "dressing".

INGREDIENTS

75g/3oz squid, cleaned
75g/3oz raw prawns
3–4 fresh scallops
½ egg white
15ml/1 tbsp cornflour, mixed with a little water
250g/9oz egg noodles
75–90ml/5–6 tbsp vegetable oil
50g/2oz mange-touts
2.5ml/½ tsp salt
2.5ml/½ tsp light brown sugar
15ml/1 tbsp Chinese rice wine or dry sherry
30ml/2 tbsp light soy sauce
2 spring onions, finely sliced
chicken stock, if necessary
few drops of sesame oil

SERVES 4

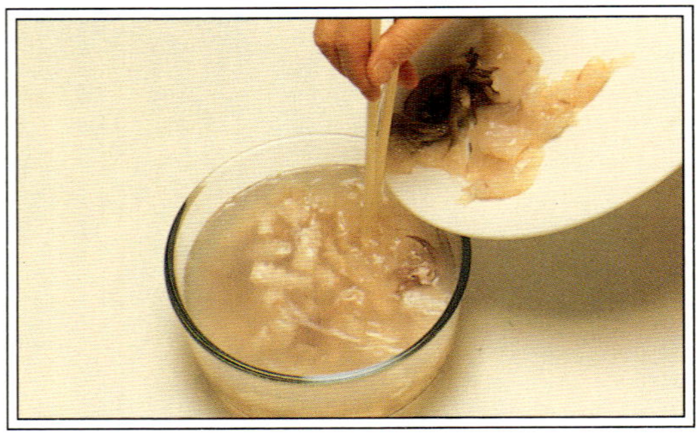

1 Open up the squid and score the inside in a criss-cross pattern. Cut the squid into 1–2.5cm/½–1in pieces and soak in boiling water until all the pieces curl up. Rinse in cold water and drain.

2 Peel the prawns and cut each in half lengthways. Cut each scallop into 3 thin slices. Mix the scallops and prawns with the egg white and cornflour paste.

3 Cook the noodles in boiling water according to the manufacturer's instructions, then drain and rinse under cold water. Mix with about 15ml/1 tbsp of the oil.

4 Heat about 15–30ml/2–3 tbsp of the oil in a wok until hot. Stir-fry the mange-touts and seafood for about 2 minutes, then add the salt, sugar, wine or sherry, half of the soy sauce and the sliced spring onions. Stir the mixture and add a little stock if necessary. Remove and keep warm.

5 Heat the remaining oil in the wok and stir-fry the noodles for 2–3 minutes with the remaining soy sauce. Place the noodles in a large serving dish and pour the seafood mixture over them. Sprinkle with a few drops of sesame oil. Either serve at once or, if you prefer, when cold.

富
貴
福

EGG FRIED RICE

Use rice with a fairly firm texture. For this dish, the rice should be boiled at least 2–3 hours before it is fried, so it can cool completely. If not, it will go soggy and the grains will not separate.

INGREDIENTS

3 eggs
5ml/1 tsp salt
2 spring onions, finely chopped
30–45ml/2–3 tbsp vegetable oil
450g/1lb cooked rice
115g/4oz peas

SERVES 4

1 In a bowl, lightly beat the eggs with a pinch of the salt and a few pieces of the spring onion.

2 Heat the oil in a saucepan or wok. When it is hot, add the egg mixture and stir and turn gently until the eggs are scrambled.

3 Add the rice and stir so that the grains are separated. Stir in remaining salt and peas. Top with remaining spring onions and serve.

NOODLES WITH VEGETABLES

This dish makes a delicious vegetarian supper on its own, or serve it as a side-dish with a main course of fish, meat or poultry.

INGREDIENTS

225g/8oz egg noodles
15ml/1 tbsp sesame oil
45ml/3 tbsp groundnut oil
2 garlic cloves, thinly sliced
2.5cm/1in piece fresh root ginger, finely chopped
2 fresh red chillies, seeded and sliced
115g/4oz broccoli, broken into small florets
115g/4oz baby sweetcorn
175g/6oz shiitake or oyster mushrooms, sliced
1 bunch spring onions, sliced
115g/4oz pok choi or Chinese cabbage, shredded
115g/4oz beansprouts
15–30ml/1–2 tbsp dark soy sauce
salt and ground black pepper

SERVES 4

1 Cook the egg noodles in a pan of boiling salted water according to the manufacturer's instructions. Drain well and toss in the sesame oil. Set aside.

2 Heat the groundnut oil in a wok or large frying pan and stir-fry the garlic and ginger for 1 minute. Add the chillies, broccoli, baby sweetcorn and mushrooms and stir-fry for a further 2 minutes.

3 Add the sliced spring onions, shredded pok choi or cabbage and the beansprouts to the wok. Stir-fry for about 2 minutes.

4 Toss in the noodles, soy sauce and black pepper. Continue to cook over a high heat for 2–3 minutes, until the ingredients are well mixed and warmed through. Serve at once.

NOODLES WITH CHICKEN, PRAWNS AND HAM

Egg noodles can be cooked up to 24 hours in advance and kept in a bowl of cold water. If you cannot find Chinese noodles, Italian pasta can be used as a substitute.

INGREDIENTS

275g/10oz dried egg noodles
15ml/1 tbsp vegetable oil
1 onion, chopped
1 garlic clove, crushed
2.5cm/1in piece fresh root ginger, peeled and chopped
50g/2oz canned water chestnuts, sliced
15ml/1 tbsp light soy sauce
30ml/2 tbsp fish sauce or strong chicken stock
175g/6oz cooked chicken breast, sliced
150g/5oz cooked ham, thickly sliced, cut into short strips
225g/8oz prawns, cooked and peeled
175g/6oz beansprouts
200g/7oz canned baby sweetcorn, drained
2 limes, cut into wedges, to garnish
1 small bunch fresh coriander, finely chopped, to garnish

SERVES 4–6

1 Cook the noodles according to the manufacturer's instructions. Drain and set aside.

2 Heat the oil in a wok. When it is hot, add the onion, garlic and ginger and stir-fry until soft. Add the chestnuts, soy sauce, fish sauce or chicken stock, chicken, ham and prawns. Stir to combine well.

3 Add the noodles, beansprouts and sweetcorn. Stir-fry for 6–8 minutes, then serve immediately with lime wedges for squeezing and garnished with coriander.

SPECIAL FRIED RICE

Special Fried Rice is an elaborate dish that is almost a meal in itself. To serve it as a light lunch or supper dish, increase the quantities of prawns and ham.

INGREDIENTS

50g/2oz cooked, peeled prawns
50g/2oz cooked ham or prosciutto
3 eggs
5ml/1 tsp salt
2 spring onions, finely chopped
60ml/4 tbsp vegetable oil
115g/4oz peas
15ml/1 tbsp light soy sauce
15ml/1 tbsp Chinese rice wine or dry sherry
450g/1lb cooked rice

1 Pat the cooked prawns dry with kitchen paper. Using a sharp knife, cut the ham or prosciutto into small dice about the same size as the peas.

2 Break the eggs into a bowl, add a pinch of the salt and a few pieces of the finely chopped spring onion. Beat the mixture lightly with a fork or a wire whisk until well combined. Set aside until needed.

3 Heat a wok, then add half the oil. When hot, add the peas, prawns and ham and stir-fry for 1 minute *(left),* then add the soy sauce and wine. Remove and keep warm.

4 Heat the remaining oil and lightly scramble the eggs. Add the rice and stir so that each grain is separated. Add the remaining salt, spring onions, prawns, ham and peas. Blend well and serve hot or cold.

SWEET AND SOUR NOODLES

Noodles combined with chicken and a selection of vegetables in a tasty sweet and sour sauce create a quick and satisfying meal.

INGREDIENTS

275g/10oz egg noodles
30ml/2 tbsp vegetable oil
3 spring onions, chopped
1 garlic clove, crushed
2.5cm/1in piece fresh root ginger, peeled and grated
5ml/1 tsp hot paprika
5ml/1 tsp ground coriander
3 boneless chicken breasts, sliced
115g/4oz mange-touts, topped and tailed
115g/4oz baby sweetcorn
225g/8oz fresh beansprouts
15ml/1 tbsp cornflour
45ml/3 tbsp soy sauce
45ml/3 tbsp lemon juice
15ml/1 tbsp sugar
45ml/3 tbsp chopped fresh coriander or spring onion tops, to garnish

SERVES 4

1 Bring a large saucepan of salted water to the boil. Add the noodles and cook according to the manufacturer's instructions. Drain, cover and keep warm.

2 Heat the oil in a wok or large frying pan. Add the spring onions and cook over a gentle heat. Mix in the garlic, ginger, paprika, ground coriander and chicken, then stir-fry for 3–4 minutes. Add the mange-touts, baby sweetcorn and beansprouts and steam briefly. Then stir in the cooked noodles.

3 Combine the cornflour, soy sauce, lemon juice and sugar in a small bowl. Add to the wok and simmer briefly to thicken. Serve garnished with chopped coriander or spring onion tops.

Avocado and Lime Ice Cream

In China, as in other parts of the world, avocados are frequently eaten as desserts. Their rich texture makes them perfect for a smooth, creamy and delicious ice cream.

Ingredients

4 egg yolks
300ml/½ pint/1¼ cups whipping cream
115g/4oz/½ cup granulated sugar
2 ripe avocados
grated rind of 2 limes
juice of 1 lime
2 egg whites
fresh mint sprigs and avocado slices, to decorate

Serves 4–6

Cook's Tip

Ice creams should be quite sweet before they are frozen since they lose some of their flavour when ice cold. Do not store ice cream for too long or ice crystals will form, which will spoil the texture.

1 Beat the egg yolks in a heatproof bowl. In a saucepan, heat the cream with the sugar, stirring it well until the sugar dissolves. As the cream rises to the top of the saucepan at the point of boiling, remove the pan from the heat.

2 Gently pour the beaten egg yolks into the scalded cream, adding them in small amounts from a height above the saucepan. This stops the mixture from curdling. Allow the mixture to cool, stirring occasionally, then chill.

3 Peel and mash the avocados until they are smooth then beat them into the chilled custard with the lime rind and juice. Check for sweetness.

4 Pour the mixture into a shallow container and freeze until slushy. Beat it well once or twice as it freezes to stop large ice crystals forming.

5 Whisk the egg whites until softly peaking and fold into mixture. Freeze until firm. Serve, decorated with mint and avocado.

PINEAPPLE BOATS

A variety of exotic fruits can be used for this fruit salad depending on what is available. Look out for mandarin oranges, star fruit, pawpaw, Cape gooseberries and passion fruit.

INGREDIENTS

75g/3oz/6 tbsp sugar
300ml/½ pint/1¼ cups water
30ml/2 tbsp stem ginger syrup
2 pieces star anise
2.5cm/1in piece cinnamon stick
1 clove
juice of ½ lemon
2 mint sprigs
1 mango
2 bananas, sliced
8 lychees, fresh or canned
225g/8oz fresh strawberries, trimmed and halved
2 pieces stem ginger, cut into sticks
1 pineapple

SERVES 4–6

1 Put the sugar, water, ginger syrup, star anise, cinnamon, clove, lemon juice and mint into a saucepan. Bring to the boil and simmer for 3 minutes. Strain into a large bowl and allow to cool.

2 Slice off both the top and bottom from the mango and peel away the outer skin. Stand the mango on one end and remove the flesh in two pieces either side of the large flat stone. Slice the flesh evenly and add to the cooled syrup. Add the bananas, lychees, strawberries and ginger to the syrup. Cover and chill until ready to serve.

3 Cut the pineapple in half lengthways. Cut out the flesh to leave two boat shapes. Cut the flesh into large chunks and place in the cooled syrup.

4 Spoon the fruit into the pineapple halves and serve. There will be enough fruit left over to refill the pineapple halves.

LIME AND LYCHEE SALAD

This mixture of fruits in a tangy lime and lychee syrup, topped with a light sprinkling of toasted sesame seeds, makes a refreshing finish to a summer meal.

INGREDIENTS

115g/4oz/½ cup caster sugar
thinly pared rind and juice of 1 lime
400g/14oz can lychees in syrup
1 ripe mango, stoned and sliced
1 eating apple, cored and sliced
2 bananas, chopped
1 star fruit, sliced (optional)
5ml/1 tsp sesame seeds, toasted

SERVES 4

1 Place the sugar in a saucepan with 300ml/½ pint/1¼ cups water and the lime rind. Heat gently until the sugar dissolves, then increase the heat and boil gently for about 7–8 minutes. Remove from the heat and leave to cool.

2 Drain the lychee juice into the lime syrup with the lime juice.

3 Place the lychees, mango, apple, bananas and star fruit, if using, in a large bowl and pour over the lime and lychee syrup *(left)*. Cover and chill for 1 hour. Remove from the fridge and ladle the fruit salad into a chilled serving bowl. Sprinkle with the toasted sesame seeds and serve.

Red Bean Paste Pancakes

If you can't find red bean paste, sweetened chestnut purée or mashed dates make good substitutes. Thin pancakes can be bought from Chinese supermarkets and frozen, or you can make your own.

Ingredients

120ml/4floz/½ cup sweetened red bean paste
8 thin pancakes
30–45ml/2–3 tbsp vegetable oil
sugar, to serve

Serves 4

Cook's Tip

Cooked pancakes can be stored in the freezer. To reheat, warm in a steamer or in a microwave.

1 Spread about 15ml/1 tbsp of the red bean paste over about three-quarters of each pancake, then roll each pancake over three or four times.

2 Heat the oil in a wok or frying pan and shallow-fry the pancake rolls until golden brown, turning once.

3 Cut each pancake roll into 3–4 pieces and sprinkle with sugar to serve.

Thin Pancakes

To make 24–30 pancakes, sift 450g/1lb/4 cups plain flour into a bowl. Slowly stir in 300ml/½ pint/1¼ cups boiling water. Add 5ml/1tsp vegetable oil and mix to a firm dough. Cover with a damp cloth and leave to stand for 30 minutes. Lightly knead the dough on a floured surface for 5–8 minutes until smooth. Divide into three. Roll each piece into a cylinder, then cut into 8–10 pieces and roll into balls. Press flat, then roll into a 15cm/6in circle. Heat a small dry pan and cook one at a time until brown spots appear on the undersides. Stack the pancakes under a damp cloth until you have cooked all of them.

ALMOND CURD JUNKET

Also known as Almond Float, this dessert is usually thickened with agar-agar or isinglass, though gelatine can also be used. It comes from eastern China.

INGREDIENTS

10g/¼oz agar-agar or isinglass or 25g/1oz gelatine powder
600ml/1 pint/2½ cups water
50g/2oz/4 tbsp sugar
300ml/½ pint/1¼ cups milk
5ml/1 tsp almond essence
fresh or canned mixed fruit salad with syrup, to serve

SERVES 4–6

1 In a saucepan, slowly dissolve the agar-agar or isinglass in half the water over a gentle heat. If using gelatine, follow the manufacturer's instructions.

2 In a separate saucepan, dissolve the sugar in the remaining water over a medium heat. Add the milk and the almond essence, blending well, but do not boil.

3 Mix the milk and sugar with the agar-agar or isinglass mixture in a large serving bowl. When cool, place in the fridge for 2–3 hours to set.

4 To serve, cut the junket into small cubes and spoon into a serving dish or into individual bowls. Then pour the fruit salad, with the syrup, over the junket.

TOFFEE APPLES

A wide variety of other fruits, such as bananas and pineapples, can be cooked in this way. Sprinkle with sesame seeds for extra crunch.

INGREDIENTS

4 firm eating apples, peeled and cored
115g/4oz/1 cup plain flour
120ml/4fl oz/½ cup cold water
1 egg, beaten
vegetable oil, for deep-frying, plus 30ml/
2 tbsp for the toffee
115g/4oz/½ cup sugar

SERVES 4

1 Cut each apple into 8 pieces. Dust each piece with a little of the flour.

2 Sift the remaining flour into a mixing bowl, then slowly add the cold water and stir to make a smooth batter. Add the beaten egg and blend well.

3 Heat the oil in a wok. Dip the apple pieces in the batter and deep-fry in batches for about 3 minutes or until golden *(left)*. Remove and drain. Heat 30ml/2 tbsp of the oil in the wok, add the sugar and stir constantly until the sugar has caramelized. Quickly add the apple pieces and blend well so that each piece of apple is coated with the "toffee". Dip the apple pieces into cold water to harden before serving.

INDEX